LITTLE BIG MOUSE

Little Big Mouse
by Maria Reyes

Printed in the United States of America

ISBN 9781613795347

www.xulonpress.com

Without faith it is impossible to be well pleasing to him, for he who comes to God must believe that he exists, and that he is a rewarder of those who seek him.

(Hebrews 11:6)

INTRODUCTION

In today's society many parent's and children are losing heart in FAITH, jobs, difficult decisions in life have become our major priority these days. Our main focus has been lost along the way Someway.. Somehow. In this book, you will be focusing on Little Big Mouse with his red wagon who is determined to seek something and not give up hope. He resembles society and the red wagon as our heart's desire. We always seek other things to make or replace our happiness but in reality, all we need is FAITH.

Little Big Mouse and his red wagon with the word FAITH...

Walking by the park, Little Big Mouse sees people enjoying time with each other.

children playing on the swings and others in the sandbox.

Children see little big mouse with his red wagon passing by the park. They asked him, "Why are you pulling a red wagon?" having the word FAITH, inside.

Little Big Mouse asked, I would like to know more about it. "Do you have faith?" Children were amazed about that question. "No," the children said, our parents never talk to us about it.

"Our parents are coming!" said the children, so we better get going. "Who are you talking to?" asked the parents. We were talking to a little mouse. What is your name? parents asked.. my name is Little Big Mouse.

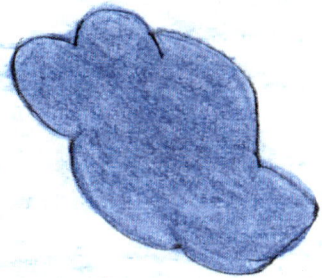

Little Big Mouse asked, "why do so some many people say they don't have time for Jesus anymore?" Learning about faith is important to us all.

Walking with a stunned look on his face, Little Big Mouse kept on going pulling his red wagon to find answers.

I'm going to the shopping mall across the street?
Said little big mouse.

"I've made it" said little big mouse. Now I can go inside the mall.

Wow, the shopping mall is big and there are children and parents. Children walking, some are eating and some buying clothes but how do I find faith, I'm very sad, said little big mouse.

Sir, "do you know about faith and how it works"? No, said the man.

People are just looking at me; I wonder why, what have I done? I just want to know about faith. Little boy, do you know about faith? No I don't.

"I don't know what you are talking about," said the little boy. You don't know what faith is, your parents don't go to church either; No, said the little boy.

I'm stunned, because of what the little boy said, Hmmm not very many children are taught by their parents. so many people are not in church not believing on what God has for them. Said little big mouse.

My heart is broken on what the people were saying, even the children. Where is the faith in there hearts.

I have to go find a church, I have to keep on looking until I find one. Said little big mouse.

Oh, there is one! and it's a big church, now I know I can find my answers here; I'm so excited that I could find a church. "Thank you Jesus."

I got to go inside this church and hear what they are preaching about.

Welcome Everyone
Services:
Wed. 7pm- Sun. 9:30am- 11am
Pastor: Benny Navarre

So little big mouse went in, and by his surprise he didn't see very many parents or children at church. I'm very sad, I just can't believe this.

Now, I remember when I was passing by the park and when I went to the shopping mall I saw them there. It Hurts me to see this, because they put other things before God instead.

Well, what matters is that I'm here to learn about faith and how it works. I'm going to the very front of the bench so I can hear what Pastor Benny is going to preach about.

Pastor Benny, by his surprise said welcome to the service. And by any chance what is your name?
My name is Little Big Mouse and brought my red wagon with me if that's okay. That's fine, said Pastor Benny.

Children of God, let's keep on talking about FAITH. Wow!, said little big mouse I'm in the right place, he is talking about faith just what I wanted to hear. I'm not leaving until it's over that is so cool. I never heard it like that, I just came in the right time.

Let's pray, for the service is over said Pastor Benny. I don't want it to be over yet, said Little Big Mouse, I want to hear and learn more about faith. I'm going to talk to the Pastor after the service.

Pastor Benny said Little Big Mouse, how can I learn more about faith? It is so exciting I want more of God's word is there anything else that I need to do so I can learn more about it. Pastor Benny said, come back next Sunday and we will continue on FAITH so I will see you then. Little Big Mouse said. I'm so excited and I am coming back.

Little Big Mouse, got stronger and stronger in faith he never gave up even though when he would face hard decisions in his life. His focus was on Jesus Christ he learned not to trust in men but on God. Now it's time to tell the people about Jesus Christ because there is not much time left. Parents and children may not want to hear about God's Word, but that is not going to stop me from telling them. I'm going to do what the word say's, preach the good news to all people.

If I have faith like a mustard seed, all things are possible. It changed me and I know that those who believe will be changed too.

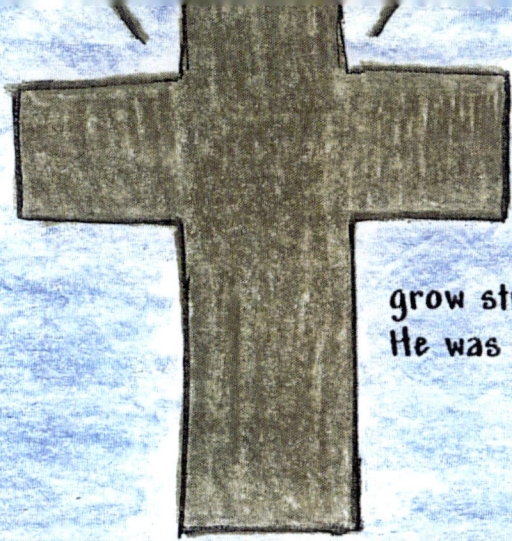

Live on His word day by day and you to will grow stronger and stronger in FAITH. Little Big Mouse believed and so can you! He was small in size but Big in faith, doesn't have to stop here..

You can receive Jesus Christ in your heart today, all you have to do is tell Jesus to forgive you of all your sins. Jesus died for you and me to have life and life eternal. One day we will be with Him in Heaven because tomorrow is not promised to us.

If you said yes, welcome into the family of Jesus Christ.
Thank you, Little Big Mouse ^^)~

FAITH

In Loving memory of Levi Martinez,
Went to be with the Lord in Oct. 08, 2010.
He was 10yrs. Old and eager to learn
more about faith. Just like Little Big Mouse
small in size but Big in Faith.

The Lord has brought me to this point that I rejoice everyday thanking him for coming into my life. From the time of my early childhood my desire was to let people know about God. I started trusting in God when I was in need spiritually, physically and financially. I noticed that many things were going right, I knew God had a big part of it. From then on He was my only Desire and the only one who would never leave me in tough times. My focus was on God, my faith also grew and brought me to believe in myself.

This book will inspire you to have FAITH and trust God knowing that all things are possible.

TO GOD BE THE GLORY

Maria Reyes

CPSIA information can be obtained
at www.ICGtesting.com
Printed in the USA
LVXC02n0139311014
411336LV00002B/2

9781613795347